Thank You

By buying this magazine, you support small business owners and small creators!

TalesOfTheGods aims to connect the metaphysical and spiritual communities.

Cover Photo - Matteo Spagnolo.

If you would like to write in anonymously, or join our team for the next edition feel free to send a email to TalesOTheGods@gmail.com

TalesOfTheGods, September 2021

TalesOfTheGods.com

- PRACTICAL WITCHCRAFT -

facebook.com/groups/665578877692886

Contributors

Desirée Goulden	Owner, layout design, contributor
Owen Lee Heavenhill	Photographer, Contributor
Dana Lee Beaudreau	Founding member, Contributor

The TalesOfTheGods & Practical Witchcraft magazine is a community project. Our roster of contributors is constantly shifting. Everyone who works on the magazine takes home an equal take of the income from the sales of this magazine.

We aim to bring education and entertainment to people of all levels of experience and paths. If you have a point of view that you would like to share with the world, feel free to reach out to join us. We are currently looking for people of colour to join us. Whether you are a teacher, or just interested in taking part, we have a place for you.

Have a shop or product you want to share with the world? Contact us and we will run a free full page ad for you in the next edition! We release on every day of the wheel of the year, so it's easy to follow release dates!

We understand that there may be some who may not want to support Amazon, so we have made the shift from publishing through Kindle Direct Publishing for our paper back editions to Ingram Spark. This will allow for wider distribution (Chapters, Barns & Noble, indie book shops) for those who want to support us without supporting Amazon and Jeff Bezos.

Please know that all opinions are that of the contributor and may not reflect the team in general.

Contents

Reflections From Owen On Religion	PAGE 2
Can Music Influence Your Magic?	PAGE 6
Tiffany Lazic's "The Great Work": a Review	PAGE 10
An Introduction to Ogham	PAGE 15
A Witch Called Karen	PAGE 18
Witch shop new illegal owner running a cult?	PAGE 20
Reddit Witches "Hex" The Taliban	PAGE 27
Altar Art	PAGE 34

 The Underworld Oracle Deck
By Desiree Goulden

25 Full colour cards

Works with reversed cards

Works with other decks

$23.99 Cad

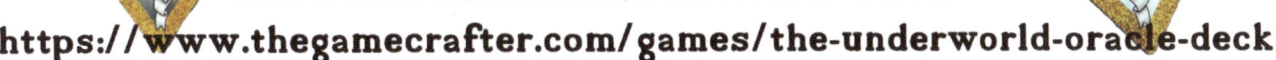

https://www.thegamecrafter.com/games/the-underworld-oracle-deck

Reflections From Owen On Religion

Before I started working with the other gods, I was at one point a christian. I was raised in the church. I have since gone back to church, and let me tell you, when the pagan goes back to church and starts working with Jesus again, things get a little weird. Questions like, "If I wanted to do communion again, but with the rest of my deities and guides instead, how would that work?" That question was after I decided I needed to make it an entire ritual, complete with baking the bread from scratch, with intention, picking out the wine.

So, to answer that question, how would one? The answer is easy, you pour for them, when you would pour for the disciples.

The day that I actually made it, I was actually surprisingly nervous. This was my first time doing communion in probably about 5 years, and to be honest, I wasn't sure if I could at first either. Meditation and reflection, and the knowledge that I don't worship any gods, I only work with them, so therefore none of them are before any of them, led me to realize that yes, I still could.

I went out that day and picked out a bottle of red wine, I don't have any advice on what I picked. I picked out a petite sirah, but really, whatever you want to drink is fine. (And, yes, grape juice, or cranberry juice, will always be a good substitute if you don't want to drink.) And when I went home, I started the bread so it could rise. As I started kneading it, I put my intentions in it.

Once the bread was rise, I put it in the oven. I kept the basics of communion (from a Methodist stand point.) the same, and added in a few of my own touches and changed a few small things to just better suit me and my spiritual path.

This all leads up a broader point though, of, part of why christianity never quite felt right to me, was because something always felt missing, like there could be something more. Piecing everything for communion together into one big ritual, like I would do with my other dieties, it didn't feel like anything was missing anymore. I do think the intention and thought I put into it really helped with what was missing.

-Owen Lee Heavenhill

Jim Two Snakes
Spiritual Advisor

 jimtwosnakes.net

 facebook.com/jimtwosnakes

 instagram.com/jimtwosnakes

 patreon.com/spiritualdad

Many people think the term Spirituality is about religion, but it doesn't have to be. In fact I think most people are Spiritual no matter if they are religious or not! Spirituality is about understanding and exploring your higher purpose, your interconnectedness to all of creation, and living authentically. It is my goal to help you feel inspired and fulfilled.

I do this by asking questions, giving suggestions, and then helping develop ways of marking progress and providing accountability. You don't have to believe the same way I, or anyone else, does. The coaching is centered around your needs and beliefs. I can't do the work for you, but I can help you with motivation and seeing things from a new perspective. Contact me now to schedule a free 15 minute initial consultation.

CONSULTATION PACKAGE

A call, a game plan, and a follow up.
One initial hour long call via Zoom, Skype or Discord
A recording of the call you can refer back to later
20 minute follow up / accountability call two weeks later

$150

TAROT READING

Divination to help guide you.
1-3 questions, submitted by email
Photos, a written report, and an audio report of your reading sent via email
48 hour turn around

$60

FIRE CEREMONY

A POWERFUL ceremony of change performed on your behalf.

You will receive instructions how to prepare for the ceremony
I will conduct the Fire Ceremony at an arranged time
You will receive a video of your ceremony, and any insights I have

$60

A POWERFUL ceremony of change performed in person for you or a group.
For individuals or groups up to ten
I will bring all needed supplies, teach you about the history of the Q'ero and the ceremony, how to participate, and then perform the ceremony
Please contact us about larger groups and gatherings

$250

SPIRITUAL CLEANSINGS

Removal of heavy energy and negativity.
For individuals, homes, or businesses.
I will bring all needed supplies.
Home cleansings can include help sorting and tidying
Rates will vary depending on number of people and/or size of house or business. Contact us for more information

---

The Best Value For Jim's Services visit
www.jimtwosnakes.net or
www.patreon.com/spiritualdad for more information

Can Music Influence Your Magic?

According to psychological research, infants are able to detect music even in the womb. It stands to reason then that music, which is found in almost every culture, has a large impact on almost every creature on the planet. Music alters our moods, influences our actions, and even plays with our creativity and imagination. If music be the food of our souls, one can take the stance that music serves as one of the more important tools when we are learning to expand and grow our abilities and our craft. (In my own opinion)

There are many ways music can be used when we are training ourselves up to the greater beings that we promise to be. Be it an Indigo Child or a Priest/Priestess or simply a Lightworker, music is a key tool that in many respects might be overlooked simply because it is so commonly used.

Music sets a mood for ceremony but depending on the type of music and its resonance it can also become a key to open doors that might otherwise be closed to us.

In meditation, the right music, uncluttered by someone else's words, can lead us to a clearer image seen through the third eye, opening us to messages that might otherwise be mistaken for daydreaming or outside noise.

In Reiki and healing practices, music is often used to mellow out the patient and unblock any doors or pipes that they may have shuttered in defense which might otherwise prevent the necessary healing that their chakra or their spirit may be barred against.

In potion making, music is often used like a stir stick to help combine and glue together the elements creating a more effective salve, tonic, or elixir.

Music has a wide base of styles and uses, and any practitioner can use it anyway they feel like using it.

We are not limited in how we call our guides or how we use our tools. Everyone's craft is different and so is everyone's skill/talent/gift. I invite you to experiment with how music might help you improve your magic and share with others what you discover there..

— *Dana Lee Beaudreau*

The Future, Regrettably
Coming Fall 2021

The debut urban fantasy novel from Desirée Goulden, prequel to the Aurora Garroway series.

Julian is a man with nothing but a name. Woken from a coma and thrust into a war he does not want to fight, he is the body guard and right hand man of a tyrannical cult leader, Rose. Escape is futile and attempts cause innocent people to be killed to keep him in line. With death as the only escape, he becomes reckless in battle, hoping to be cut down and finally escape the life he is trapped in.

Rose notices and offers him a boon: stay in line and do as she says and he will be able to visit the future in his dreams. He will be able to live a comfortable life and see why the Conduit Hierarchy's war is just, and how it will better the world.

Will this be enough to pacify Julian? Or will this motivate him to tear down the organization that seeks to control him, and find the truth?

@inkwood_tarot   @InkwoodJournal

inkwoodtarot.com

Inkwood Tarot - Readings by Cynthia: tarot reader, empath, certified Reiki practitioner and ordained Pagan clergy.

" I offer tarot readings by phone, video call and seasonally in-person at local events, festivals and shops. With over 20 years of tarot study and experience, I love helping people bring harmony, balance and success to their lives. Join me in exploring your ultimate potential!"

To learn more or schedule a reading visit:
http://inkwoodtarot.com

Tiffany Lazic's "The Great Work": a Review

For many of you who are just starting out on your journey or who are looking for a way to expand you base, The Great Work by Tiffany Lazic is a great place to start. The Great Work is a day by day growing experience which provides the reader with daily exercises to help them grow in their craft and enables them to explore or discover new areas of the arts without needing to invest large amounts of time or expense to find out if it's a good fit. Written without any particular spirit guide or deity in mind, the information and daily assignment help you simply and slowly explore different areas of yourself and you craft. Exploring a number of fields including Reiki, healing, tarot, rune reading, and meditation, the reader can choose to discover whether the skills involved are of an interest, calling or fit for them. If you have only recently discovered your gift or are unsure about your gift and how to use it, this book provides many small bits of homework to be done each day that have been designed to help you become more acquainted with yourself and your gift. It is also divided into sections dedicated to many of the skills, or gifts that you may want to explore going so far as to explain many of the crafts that some may not even be aware of. This book, designed to be a year long journey of learning, growing and exploration, makes it easy to try out new things or dig a little deeper into those abilities that you have only scratched the surface into opening. I highly recommend reading this if you are just starting out or looking for a way to expand your craft base.

Tiffany Lazic is the owner of The Hive and Grove Centre for Holistic Wellness and a graduate of Transformational Arts College of Spiritual Healing as a Spiritual Psychotherapist.

— *Dana Lee Beaudreau*

(Lazic, 2015)

References

Lazic, T. (2015). the Great Work: Self-Knowledge and Healing Through the Wheel of the Year. In T. Lazic, the Great Work: Self-Knowledge and Healing Through the Wheel of the Year. Woodbury, MN: Llewellyn Publication, Llewellyn Worldwide Ltd.

"Fusing ancient Western spirituality, energy work, and psychology, The Great Work is a practical guide to personal transformation season by season. Learn to be truly holistic by incorporating key physical, emotional, and energetic practices into your life at times when the natural tides are in harmony with your process.

The Great Work captures the core essence of each festival with eight key themes that span the annual cycle—a cycle that reflects human development and experience. Discover how Yule can alleviate a painful childhood, how Beltane can facilitate conscious relationships, and how Mabon can assist with determining your life's purpose. Find guidance through daily journal questions, elemental meditations, and the author's unique energy-healing technique of Hynni. With this invaluable resource for your journey of inner alchemy, you'll develop an intimate connection with the earth's impulse to create balance and harmony." - Amazon store page.

Paperback: $32.26
Kindle: $ 28.71
Purchase:
https://amzn.to/39ahtQi

TOTG Merch!

We have new additions to the TalesOfTheGods.com merch page!

This is a back and white illustration of Achilles and Patroclus with a rainbow background and a inscription that reads: "No dude, they were totally just really good friends!" -Very Smart People.

Buy at **https://tales-of-the-gods-2.creator-spring.com/listing/achilles-and-patroclus-being-b**

$44.17 $6.20 $31.54

Christina & Martin

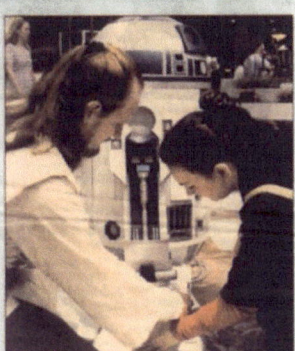
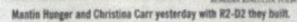

✉ carrhunger@carrhunger.com
📷 www.instagram.com/Carrhunger/
f www.facebook.com/carrhunger/

Meeting at a Dr Who convention in Toronto in 1987, Christina and Martin have, combined, over 62 years experience in the entertainment industry.

Accumulating such titles as Camera, Editing, Tape Operator, Director, Actor, Writer, Costumes, Props Builders, AD, Fight Coordinator, etc and so on... their experiences are broad and diverse BUT they still, to this day, love bringing the joy of building props, education on the industry and the popular process of Cosplay to conventions and events. X-Men, Cody Banks, Total Recall 2070, Scooby Doo, Stargate, Star Trek, FX The Series, EFC, Flash, Arrow, Legends of Tomorrow, are only a few of the productions on their list of experiences.

Stage, Live Performances, Characters at Festivals, add to their range of talents. Come experience their love of sharing knowledge, their skills and stories of their experiences.

An Introduction to Ogham

A long time ago Druids used a secret language to communicate and perform their ceremonies. This language was so secret that rather than write it down, it was passed along from generation to generation by word of mouth. It was many centuries later before it was first written down on stones (we call these runes) and wooden sticks, called staves (known as Ogham).

Consisting of twenty letters in four sets of five letters or symbols, these are inscribed on trees native to Ireland. The first three sets consist of consonants and the last set is made up of vowels. These were arranged to communicate in a secret language used only by those trained up to this purpose.

These days, students of ogham are taught instead how to respectfully use these runic inscriptions to decipher situations and read the energies effecting a person's predestined path.

How to read Ogham:
The staves are gathered together and stored in a velvet or specially prepared bag. The reader calls upon their guide to lead the client or subject to reveal themselves in the staves. The individual (or the reader on their behalf) reaches into the bag and withdraws three staves. These staves are inscribed with symbols that relate to various trees. Trees much like flowers each have their own meaning and thus are able to communicate with us.

The first stave drawn is the Ray of Knowledge. This is the influence that the past has on the subject. It may represent the events surrounding the subject and how they are manipulating or being manipulated by the subject.

The second stave is the Ray of Peace. This stave represents the foundation of the present or what is influencing the subject now. This position represents intelligence. Here we see what is the undercurrent of the events that are unfolding. What is at the root of things.

The final stave drawn is the Ray of Power. This stave speaks to the future of events as they are unfolding. It represents the potential for change and the movement of energy in the subject's pilgrimage. Our third position is the magic box. The gift or message which is being bestowed on us in order to step into the answers or quest we are now encountering.

There are two spreads that we are familiar with.

The Awen which is used to examine knowledge, peace, and power. It speaks with the Land/Sea/Sky or Earth/Water/Air.
The Welsh Triad which mainly focuses on the event, intelligence, and the god's influence. You begin with a Bridge which carries down to a vine and follows into the event line of thinking and examination.

Either spread will answer the same basic questions.

While I could go into what all the trees, runes and symbols are holding in significance, I think it would be better if you are interested in further study into Ogham reading that you seek out books that are more in depth than this basic introduction.
I will leave you with this one taste. Mistletoe is a parasite and therefore it is all powerful. Should mistletoe appear in your reading be very cautious. Its influence may be more than you can handle.

— Dana Lee Beaudreau

Simply Magical Audio!

Want something magical to listen to? Here are a selection of some of out favourite practicioner made podcast and music! From good jams to great podcasts, these creators give hours of education and art!

The Guide Your Soul podcast is a new podcast with great potential! Mary Fellows talks about anything and everything through a spiritualist point of view.

She is a respected healer and spiritual teacher who you should keep your eye on.

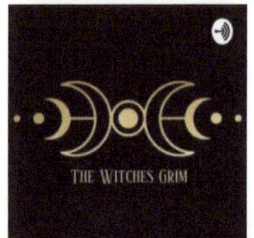

A great podcast lead by two experienced practitioners. You will always learn something new from this podcast and is great to listen to throughout your day.

Grab some tea and curl up with your favourite knitted blanket and give this a listen!

Selki Girl brings the nostalgic vibes of the 2000s with a hint of magic. Her album "For The Profane" gained some traction with some scandalous tales of it causing one to astral project. People seemed to make up tall tales about this album and from listening to it, it's not hard to see why. While it wont make you astral project, it is a experience that shouldn't be missed!

An oldie but a goody. Some of my favourite songs from my teen years where written by him.

This bard weaves magic in his words and story telling and music and will forever be an adored musician in the Pagan world.

A Witch Called Karen

The internet has shed light on no small number of obnoxious, racist, older, white women in recent years. With everyone having a phone on them at all times, it is becoming increasingly difficult for people to act like a fool in public and get away with it. While the name "Karen" usually denotes an entitled, older, white, Christian conservative throwing a hissy fit over people just existing around her, entitledness is as always: intersectional.

We have seen Karens of all shapes, sizes, ages, and colours and has seemed to move from the stereotypical bottle blonde churchgoer to anyone with an entitled attitude, loud mouth, and arrogant disposition. It seems now, that one of our own has been bestowed the title of "Karen."

On August 24th I came across a video from the TikTok creator tizzyent who duetted a video of a woman being harassed by a screaming harpy on an electric scooter. The woman on the scooter rides around in frantic and rapid movements while screaming "Ugly Packie fuck get out of my path!" as she blocks the road for the woman trying to cross it.

As the video stated, this took place at Port Perry Waterfront, Ontario Canada. According to IBTimes she continues on to harass people who intervene and stop her from attacking the family. The original post was made by @_rabioli on TikTok who was the victim of the hate. Apparently, the woman disliked her race, as well as her clothes.

When the woman called her a witch in a derogatory but less rude version of "bitch", she turns and states that she is in fact a witch, and the girl "knows nothing about witches". Apparently, this is a common theme with the Witch Of The Wheelchair, and this is not the first time she has caused trouble in the neighborhood. Although we have not been able to dig up her name, we have found out the stores in the area have nearly all banned her from shopping there, so it is unlikely that she will be causing trouble there for a while.

By her admission, she is a witch and the victim has "no idea what that means." She claiming to be one of us, leaves a bad taste in many in the communities mouths, as well as a stain on our name. While I do not condone harassment, doxing, or anything of the sort, accountability must be held. Our community is small and any bad apple can ruin the bunch. If you have any information about this woman, please contact us at TalesOTheGods@gmail.com, or through our CONTACT page. If she is in any circle, gathering, group, or moot of yours, it may be worthwhile to have a chat about her conduct and how it affects the entire community. Remember, much of western spirituality and magical practice is influenced or comes from people that have different races, clothes, religions, and practices. Our differences strengthen us and build the community. There is no place for racism here.

-Desirée Gouldem

A SHOP OR A CULT?

Metaphysical and Witch shops are the cornerstone for the occult and spiritual communities. They give us tools, knowledge, and services as well as a sense of community where we are usually surrounded by people who don't share our religious and magical beliefs. They can make or break the local community, especially if they are the only one in a certain area. I would say if there is one thing that almost all of us hold sacred it is the local Witch shop.

(Please know that all claims are allegations until proven true in a court of law. Much of what comes from this article is first-hand experiences from people in and around the business, customers, and that which is public information.)

This is why I was dismayed to see that one such Witch shop has become more a thinly veiled cult than a servant of the community. While interacting in one of the many Witchy groups I am a part of on FaceBook, I came across a post asking for more metaphysical shops in South Carolina because the store has gone downhill since new management. She claims that the new owner has admitted to selling "defective merchandise" and blaming the customer for the product. She also claims that they knowingly stock and sell white supremacist content there, and bullied one of the workers until he quit because he was gay.

Hey I'm looking for some good places to buy supplies from. My local shop (Canterbury Emporium) has just completely gone down hill under their new management. The new owner has admitted to knowingly sell defective merchandise and when people would call and ask about what was wrong with their products the owner would tell them that is wasn't the product, something must have gone wrong with the spell and sell more of the defective item to them KNOWING what was truly wrong. Not to mention all the lies she's been telling customers to get them to buy more stuff. AND knowingly being affiliated/ stocking white supremacy merchandise. She even bullied my friend until he was fired because he's gay. I can't support this. They're the only local store that sells occult supplies and I would hate to have to order off Amazon. So if anyone has any good online suppliers, please help a girl out. This woman does NOT deserve to stay in business let alone take my money.

All names will be protected for the protection of the people who have brought it to light, so let's call the person who brought this up, Anon. When I saw Anon's post, I was intrigued and approached them to ask if she would give me a bit more information for a new article for the website. What I expected was to find someone with little to no actual proof, and to walk away with some gossip and nothing to write about. What I found was the beginnings of a cult, a woman who legally should not be in charge of a business, a business that is in decline, and so many red flags that even rose coloured glasses could stop you from seeing them.

So what is going on with Canterbury Emporium?

Canterbury Emporium LLC was Canterbury Cloak and Dagger until January 1st, 2021. We don't know why but from what we understand, the original owner (Christina Crider) wanted to either lessen the load of the shop on her or get a business partner. We don't know why, but considering Covid has affected us all, and especially small businesses, that is not surprising. Unfortunately, the person who heard the call for help had less than charitable motives.

Enter Elizabeth Donovan and the beginning of the downfall of Canterbury Emporium. Elizabeth, 36 was allegedly brought on to co-own the store, but from get-go there was trouble in paradise when Christina found out she would not be the owner on paper. Why would that be?

Because Elizabeth has charges for a DUS (driving under suspension), a simple possession charge (Marijuana), and a DUI wherein she allegedly hit a police car. Anon tells us that because of this that she can not have a business license... which is problematic as the reason she was brought on was specifically to be the new owner so that Christina could bow out of the store.

So concerned was Christina in finding someone that she did not perform a background check on Elizabeth and it managed to bite her in the butt almost immediately. On top of Elizabeth not being able to have a business license because of her charges, her credit is apparently so terrible she can't even be put on any of the business accounts. They agreed on a 50/50 partnership and things started going downhill.

Anon paints a picture of a schoolyard bully made a boss. From day one, Elizabeth would harass and bully Christina to get her way. At one point, Christina wanted to install cameras for the protection of her staff from Elizabeth. Apparently, Elizabeth had a nasty habit of ignoring her duties.

She would ask if she could help customers then walk off and ignore them on a constant basis, as well as apparently being rather judgmental to anyone who was obviously new to the craft. This can be backed up by some of the negative reviews you can find on Google (All within the last year and sullying the nearly 5 star rating it once had, mind you.)

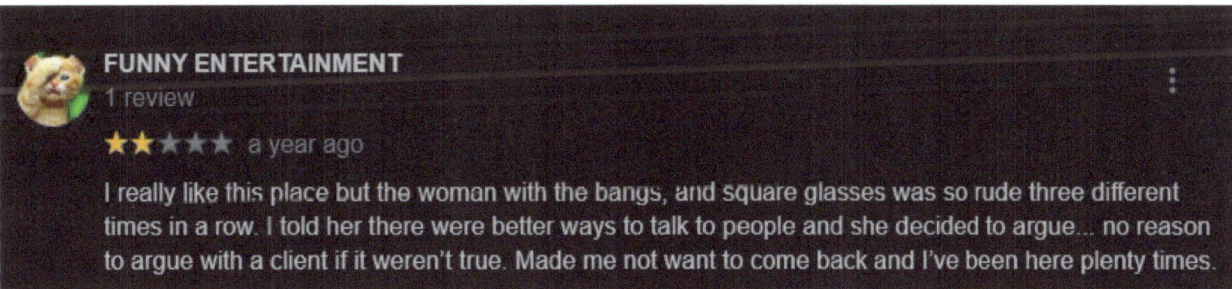

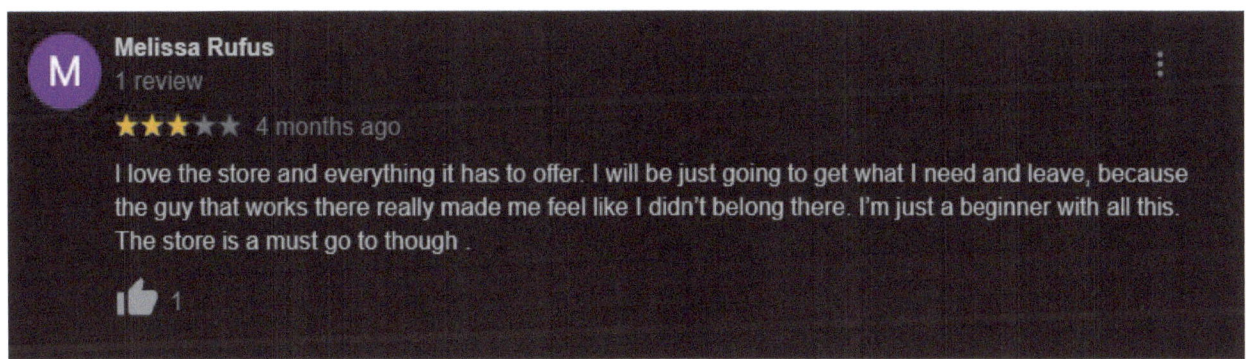

Anon explains that Elizabeth constantly is at odds with workers who were there before she got involved because they would constantly correct her false information regarding the craft. It's not that she is new to her craft either, as she allegedly brags about constantly using manipulation spells on people around her including her significant other. She has apparently said she asks your big 3 zodiac signs not out of curiosity, but so that she can assess how easily she can control you based on them.

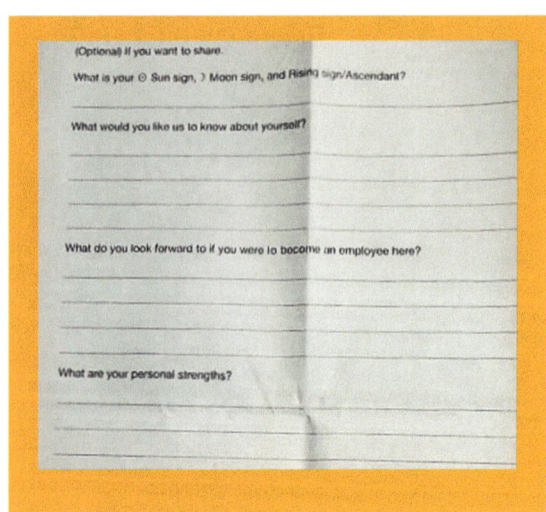

These manipulation spells and need for control has caused more than a few people to make sure to not leave any personal items at the store, lest the woman uses them in a spell which she allegedly admitted to doing before. Our sources claim that Canterbury Emporium is the only metaphysical shop in the town, meaning they ought to play an important part in the local community. Unfortunately, our sources have given us the image of the beginnings of a cult.

One of the key points on the BITE model (a way to identify cult mentality and abusive religious structures) is information control, and Elizabeth has an iron grip on the magical information coming in and going out of the Emporium. Anon tells us that Elizabeth purposely does not hire priestesses or people of authority within the magical community, and goes out of her way to hire "Baby Witches" (extremely new practitioners) so that she can continue to lie to the customers about the products they offer. The workers that are there from before she took over and are knowledgeable are constantly getting in trouble for "disrespecting" Elizabeth when they were correcting the misinformation Elizabeth gave to the clientele. Workers who have no history of problems under Christina are now coming under constant fire by Elizabeth as she attempts to push her own narrative, though what that narrative is we have no idea yet.

Our sources say that Elizabeth has admitted to only being in it for the money, but seems to be unenthused in actually putting the real effort into it. Allegedly, one of Elizabeth's duties is to control the social media accounts and all things online, however, when the reviews were shown to our sources, they reagreed that the responses sound more like Christina than Elizabeth. They have a Instagram, TikTok, and FaceBook but they seem half-assed

- at best which is is sad considering if you have a strong media presence, you can take your shop from just a shop to a full-on media icon. Witch shops on TikTok have thousands of followers and fans from across the world, not just their local community. Take, for example, Catland Books in New York.

Run by Bee Hollywood, br00klynwitch is the TikTok about Bee and their Witch shop, Catland Books. They have 188 thousand followers and over 2 million collective likes on their videos, and their social media presence has made them a very well-known name in the witchy community.

While not uploading every day, they bring flavor and entertainment to their video series "Wild ass phone calls while working at a witch shop". These videos bring an approachable, funny, and interesting look into the day-to-day workings of the shop, and give the vibe of a sitcom taking place in a metaphysical store.

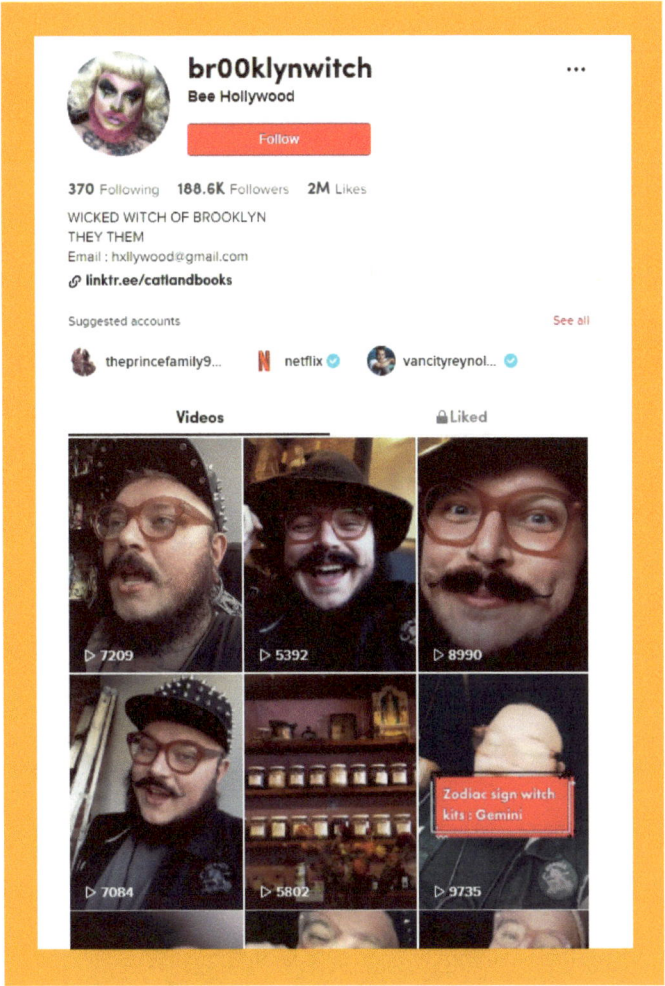

This is to say, it is not terribly difficult to create a relevant social media presence, and you would think that Elizabeth would be able to do more than a video kissing an amethyst geode. Maybe this is just me nitpicking, but if you are going to try to manipulate an entire community, and especially the young practitioners therein, you'd think a bit more effort would be put into it.

Because no shit show is complete without white supremacy, of course, she has begun stocking the shelves with content by known white supremacists. Until they were called out for it. For a time they stocked the book Futhark, a handbook of rune magic by Edred Thorsson, an alias for Stephen E. Flowers. MrFlowers is a renowned white supremacist and is part of the Asatru Folk Assembly, a white supremacist heathen organization. He is known for distorting the information in his books with a neo-satanic ideals and philosophy, and his publishing house closed and he was sued by his business partner.

While they did take the book out of the shop, but you have to wonder how they didn't catch that as Flowers is a decently well-known person for his problematic tendencies. I feel like if Christina was in charge completely that would have never happened. If Elizabeth wasn't so retaliatory against people correcting her information, she would have been told about this. I want to give her the benefit of the doubt that Elizabeth just didn't know, but considering that she doesn't seem to be new to her craft, as well as the fact that there are 838 tracked hate groups in the US, 20 of them being in South Carolina, I am doubtful that it was not an intentional push to see what the community would allow. There are 2 white supremacist organizations in Summerville alone, those being Renaissance Horizon and Patriotic Flag, both being white supremacist organizations. That is of course only personal opinion, so take that with a grain of salt, but it seems in conjunction with everything else to be a little too fishy for me.

We can't get confirmation of the claims of homophobic harassment, for obvious reasons many within the shop refuse to answer questions and put their jobs on the line, but considering these sort of supremacist organizations very often have homophobic sentiment as well, I would personally take Anon's claims at her word.

Elizabeth is coasting off the reputation of Canterbury Cloak and Dagger, actively ruining the store, manipulating and hurting people who work under her, is only in it for the money, giving faulty products and spells, and when they doing work as advertised, she blames the customer. Canterbury Emporium as it is is starting to go majorly downhill, and I believe that unless they get rid of Christina, it is going to devolve into a local cult and is going to actively hurt the local community,

If you are in Summerville and are looking for a new shop, here are some local shops, and some online to help you get what you need without supporting a white supremacist, alleged homophobe, and subpar and faulty products and spells.

Summerville Metaphysical Stores

Botanica De La Gitana - 106 E Doty Ave, Summerville, SC 29483

Online Metaphysical Stores

Grove and Grotto - Affordable metaphysical and Witchy supplies

The Quirky Cup Collective - Books, tarot decks, journals, misc

All That Shimmerzz - Crystals

-Desirée Gouldem

A Witch Called Karen

WitchTok is by far the laughing stock of the online witching world at this point. Between their creators attempting to claim Tarot cards are a closed Romani practice, to hexing the moon, fae, Artemis, Apollo, etc. From the "hex" videos from Fluffy Bunnies and "Baby Witches" sticking random things into lemons to the song Bottom Of The River by Delta Ray, to the forming of the "Reality Shifting" into anime, causing hundreds of kids to fall into maladaptive daydreaming, nobody is surprised they have played into the hands of the Reddit trolls.

R/BewitchTheTaliban is a forum on the website, Reddit, a message board website, and self-proclaimed "Front page of the internet". Reddit has come into the limelight and gained popularity over the years, drawing in a wide range of people because of it's community-generated and shared content. As it appeals to such a large amount of people, it does tend to attract Trolls and people who just want to start chaos in other parts of the internet. It is unclear whether R/BewitchTheTaliban was originally a Troll board or not. The first signs of this board was inside the R/Witchcraft forum via a post made by u/Cogito_Ergo_Sum1

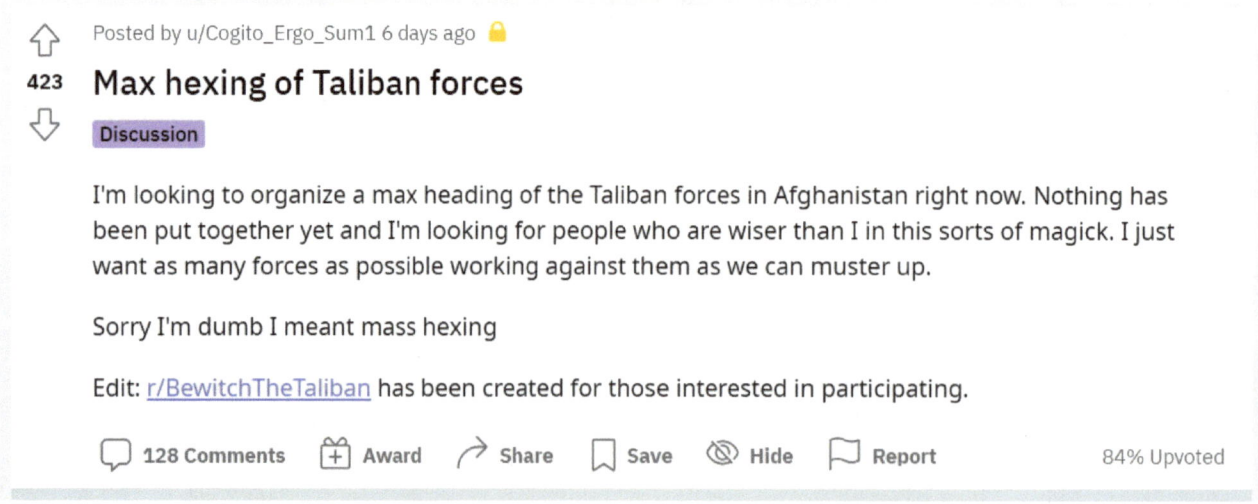

Cogito_Ergo_Sum1 has an interesting history of posting. Their account was made on November 25th, 2020. Reddit allows you to scroll through people's posts and comments and it is obvious this person has been somewhat of a Troll since they opened their account. They moderate 2 groups those being R/BewitchTheTaliban and R/HexTheTaliban.

Many of their posts that aren't related to the two groups are flagged and deleted. Some of these posts include: Israel and Covid-19 (Removed for "A variety of reasons") in R/ConspiracyTheories, and A Prophecy of Hermes in the Asclepius (Removed for spam) in R/Occult. They post at length about their drug use, in both R/Psychedelics and other unrelated forums. They ask about "how much blood makes you native" and if they can do sacred native practices. They ask about working with Isis, while also claiming to work with Paimon, and claims to be a new witch.

While I have no doubt Cogito_Ergo_Sum1 is a Troll account, with anti-Islamic sentiment, and the R/HexTheTaliban containing the first post of a naked man offering up his... orifice, a hybrid human-washing machine, and a post just saying "AAAAAAAAAAAAAAAAA", the same can not be said for those who have fallen into their R/BewitchTheTaliban forum.

In the original post, you can see people in the comments saying things like:

"I'm perfectly willing to join in but I think the word you're looking for is curse lol... I may be wrong but hexes are generally considered less severe, and since it's the Taliban we're talking about...."

"You will need to summon and gain the favor of a God of War for this one"

"I work with Freyja, sounds like a cause she would definitely get behind."

"Athena for sure. Definitely not Ares"

There are paragraphs upon paragraphs about protections, how to curse, who to curse, who to protect, who to invoke, how to invoke them and while reading I can't help but think... this sounds a lot like prayer warriors who don't actually donate or help or do anything in times of crisis, but say platitudes of "I'll pray for you".

But what is the actual forum in question like? Well... let these screenshots speak for themselves.

> Posted by u/Castlefree43 5 days ago
>
> **You'd be surprised what could be done if Israel just put 5% of their energy into bringing peace to the Middle East -- All they need to do is begin talks of it in the region and you'll see what can get done when it's done right**
>
> If you don't believe me, that's fine but I know it's time for Israel's leaders to begin the process.
>
> It will be rocky at first but it has to start somewhere, and if they do try it, please be supportive of them as this is a huge step for humanity, should it happen.
>
> When Israel's leaders (whether this generation's, the next's, or one in the future) put their energy and consciousness into bringing peace in that region, you will see great change. It's just that their current leadership wants to continue warring, hating, etc - just like the Middle Easterners - but the Israeli's have a far greater ability within them to begin the peace making process.
>
> I know people don't think it's possible because of what we've seen in the past, but that is exactly the kind of thinking that stops this from going forward. This idea that things will always remain the same, so they have to just clamp down and win, but that's not working so it's time to try for something else.
>
> The younger generation of Israeli's (and their children, and so on) will understand this intuitively but it would still help to get Israel's current leadership to consider it at least as a possibility.
>
> 89 Comments · Award · Share · Save · Hide · Report · 72% Upvoted

There are some posts I can't track down, likely they were deleted after TikTok got a hold of them.

Some of these include warning people against fighting Allah in the Astral alone, generally just hexing Hallah, and warnings to be careful when hexing the Taliban.

There is a concerning mix of people in this group, both Trolls and young practitioners who actually want to do this. Unfortunately what was contained to Reddit, was spread like a wildfire by people on TikTok who lack critical thinking skills and know to just ignore the small group of fools and racists. Witchtokers spread screenshots across the app which currently hosts the largest online group of witches, pagans, and practitioners.

"Baby Witches" (A new more derogatory infantilizing term for new practitioners, usually similar to Fluffy Bunnies) saw a way to show how "powerful" they are to their audiences on TikTok and while most people decried the stupidity of the group, some Baby Witches joined the "fight" to "hex the Taliban".

There has been a constant buzz since this started on August 17th and has left a bad taste in my, and many other's mouths. The Trolls aside, the underlying feeling of racism, islamophobia, and xenophobia is obvious.

Let's get something very clear for the younger audiences who may not remember 9/11. This want to get back at the Taliban for what happened in Afghanistan does:

1) Absolutely nothing. Your spellwork will do nothing, you can barely cast a circle let alone "hex" a giant group of extremists whom you don't know anything of.

2) Spread blatant and harmful islamophobia by "Attempting to kill/hex/curse Allah."

3) Shows that you don't actually want to do anything to help by donations and pushing your government officials to allow and help refugees into your country to seek refuge.

4) Shows your obvious performative activism at best, and your islamophobia at worse.

There are many Muslim countries, peoples, and traditions, some of which hold the title of "Witch" themselves. Islam is the 2nd most popular religion in the world with 1.907 Muslims around the world. (24.9% of the world's religion.) The idea that you would want to kill Allah is hateful of the people that follow him. You're looking at a tragedy that sets back women's rights in the middle east by 20 years, marks the loss of the long battle between the people of Afghanistan, and the Taliban. This is a terrible situation which we will be dealing with the fallout of for decades to come.

People are suffering, and rather than helping, some people in the Witch community are taking the piss, or actively using the conflict for clout and to spread hate.

While the Trolls started this, Baby Witches and in particular WitchTok has managed to spread a wave of hate and are actively making fools of Witches worldwide by their constant spreading of something that should have lived and died on Reddit. I understand that this will lead to this spreading of this, but I feel like people need to know how this started, and how illegitimate of a movement this is.

If you want to ACTUALLY help, and not contribute to the performative activism of "Hex the Taliban and kill Allah" Here are some links you can donate to.

https://give.unhcr.ca/page/86611/donate/1?ea.tracking.id=SEM21_AFG&utm_campaign=CA_PS_EN_AFS&gclid=CjwKCAjw64eJBhAGEiwABr9o2AC-VeuMiVPa3GeNjGa7MgUNc4UWUUEa2ooXcwpVPOrbIPHB0ufv7hoCIYUQAvD_BwE&gclsrc=aw.ds

https://secure.unicef.ca/page/88400/donate/1?ea.tracking.id=21DIEM11GSE&gclid=CjwKCAjw64eJBhAGEiwABr9o2F5_J98FYM7DrSoJRi9Yqo_2uuHBAWcrpqjlMKzhgnGC_H6qzSCpnRoCdsQQAvD_BwE

https://www.savethechildren.org/us/where-we-work/afghanistan

https://donate.unhcr.org/int/en/afghanistan-situation

https://help.rescue.org/donate-ca/afghanistan

—Desirée Gouldem

The Law Of Hospitality
Xenia - ξενία

Do not turn away your guests, be it strangers or friends.

Welcome your guest warmly into your house, invite them to stay, show them the house.

Allow to use the bath and change into clean cloths.

Ask how you may help your guest.

Provide them with a good meal, gifts, and aid to reach their next destination if needed.

Do not ask invasive questions until they are clean and have eaten.

Guests may not be a burden to their hosts, do not threaten, harm nor steal from them.

Guests are to provide the hose with stories and news of the wider world and welcome them into their own home in the future.

Follow these rules and honour the gods for Zeus, Xenios, watches over and protects travellers near and far.

www.ingramcontent.com/pod-product-compliance
Lightning Source LLC
Chambersburg PA
CBHW042255100526
44589CB00002B/23